MW00677838

Just Retrievers

HALF-PINT EDITION

Ducks Unlimited, Inc.

Memphis, Tennessee

and

Willow Creek Press

Minocqua, Wisconsin

Half-pint edition published in 2000 by Willow Creek Press.

Text and compilation copyright © 1997 by Ducks Unlimited, Inc., One Waterfowl Way, Memphis, Tennessee 38120.

Author: Chuck Petrie
Photography editor: Diane Jolie
Book Design: Dit Rutland

Half-pint edition published by Willow Creek Press, Minocqua, Wisconsin
ISBN 1-57223-390-7

Original edition published August 1997 by Ducks Unlimited

Printed in Canada

DUCKS UNLIMITED CALL TO ACTION

The success of Ducks Unlimited hinges upon each member's personal involvement in the conservation of North America's wetlands and waterfowl. You can help Ducks Unlimited meet its conservation goals by volunteering your time, energy, and resources; by participating in our conservation programs; and by encouraging others to do the same. To learn more about how you can make a difference for the ducks, call 1-800-45-DUCKS.

Cataloging in Publication Data (original edition)

Petrie, Chuck
    Just retrievers / Chuck Petrie.
        p.   cm.
    ISBN 1-57223-126-2 (hc)
    1. Retrievers. 2. Retrievers--Pictorial works.   I. Title.
SF429.R4P48   1997
636.752'7--dc21   97-33287
                                                                CIP

DUCKS UNLIMITED, INC.

The mission of Ducks Unlimited is to fulfill the annual life cycle needs of North American waterfowl by protecting, enhancing, restoring and managing important wetlands and associated uplands. Since its founding in 1937, DU has raised more than $1.3 billion, which has contributed to the conservation of over 8.8 million acres of prime wildlife habitat in all fifty states, each of the Canadian provinces, and in key areas of Mexico. In the U.S. alone, DU has helped to conserve over 1.6 million acres of waterfowl habitat. Some 900 species of wildlife live and flourish on DU projects, including many threatened and endangered species.

int edition published in 2000 by Willow Creek Press.
xt and compilation copyright © 1997 by Ducks Unlimited, Inc., One
fowl Way, Memphis, Tennessee 38120.

e copyrights to all photographs in this book belong to the photogra-
and no reproduction of the photographic images contained herein
e made without the express written permission of the photographers.

or: Chuck Petrie
graphy editor: Diane Jolie
Design: Dit Rutland

int edition published by Willow Creek Press, Minocqua, Wisconsin
1-57223-390-7

al edition published August 1997 by Ducks Unlimited

d in Canada

Cataloging in Publication Data (original edition)

Petrie, Chuck
    Just retrievers / Chuck Petrie.
      p. cm.
    ISBN 1-57223-126-2 (hc)
      1. Retrievers. 2. Retrievers--Pictorial works.   I. Title.
SF429.R4P48 1997
636.752'7--dc21   97-33287
                                                  CIP

KS UNLIMITED CALL TO ACTION

uccess of Ducks Unlimited hinges upon each member's personal
vement in the conservation of North America's wetlands and water-
You can help Ducks Unlimited meet its conservation goals by volun-
g your time, energy, and resources; by participating in our conservation
ms; and by encouraging others to do the same. To learn more about
ou can make a difference for the ducks, call 1-800-45-DUCKS.

DUCKS UNLIMITED, INC.

The mission of Ducks Unlimited is to fulfill the annual life cycle needs of North American waterfowl by protecting, enhancing, restoring and managing important wetlands and associated uplands. Since its founding in 1937, DU has raised more than $1.3 billion, which has contributed to the conservation of over 8.8 million acres of prime wildlife habitat in all fifty states, each of the Canadian provinces, and in key areas of Mexico. In the U.S. alone, DU has helped to conserve over 1.6 million acres of waterfowl habitat. Some 900 species of wildlife live and flourish on DU projects, including many threatened and endangered species.

Just Retriever[s]

HALF-PINT EDI[TION]

Ducks Unlimited, Inc.
Memphis, Tennessee
and
Willow Creek Press
Minocqua, Wisconsin

To my wife, Mary, son Geoffrey, and daughters Beth and Heidi—and to the retrievers with whom we've shared our lives: Keyni, Baxter, and Gunnar . . .

. . . and to Gene Hill, who always said it best

INTRODUCTION

Lexicographer: a writer of dictionaries, a harmless drudge.

——Samuel Johnson (1709-1784),
English lexicographer and author

Retriever. The Merriam-Webster dictionary, bequeathed to us by American lexicographer Noah Webster, defines this simple term, as it relates to dogs, as: "one that retrieves; esp: a dog of any of several breeds . . . having a heavy water-resistant coat and used esp. for retrieving game." We know, of course, that retrievers are much more than that. We know it would take an entire book to define the true essence of what retrievers are and what they mean to those of us who've been fortunate enough to claim one as a cherished companion.

Which is what this book intends to do. Webster may provide a definition, but it's one without soul. "Retriever" is more than a simple noun. A retriever has spirit, a force and vitality that radiate in our presence, and later, after we've shared a part of our life with one and he or she is gone, lives on in our hearts. The bonds we form with Maggie or Sam or Sally or Max are indelible. If you've owned more than one retriever, you know, too, that each will remain unique in your memory. Another bone to pick with Webster: ". . . and used esp. for retrieving game." Hell, they'll retrieve anything. Including game, certainly, but not to the exclusion of sticks, cans, training dummies, newspapers, slippers, fish, cats, other dogs, lost children, misplaced items, and, in police work, contraband and criminals.

Not an all-inclusive list by any means, but you get the picture.

Nor do two lines in a dictionary do justice to the breeds of retrievers that have volumes written about them; that have Web sites devoted to them; that execute in field and bench trials; that work as guide dogs for the blind; as bomb sniffers; as body recovery specialists; as guard dogs and hunting retrievers; and who have bumper stickers and countless personalized license plates displaying their names. Indeed, query the average passerby and he or she will sooner place the name "Labrador retriever" than they will "Noah Webster."

But to be fair, more people consort with retrievers on a regular basis than they do with dictionaries. At last count, for the sixth consecutive year, the Labrador retriever remained the most popular dog in American Kennel Club registry entries. The gold-en retriever ranked fourth. Out of 140 breeds recognized by the club, that's quite a testimonial to retrievers' popularity. And that's only one canine registry and only rankings for goldens and Labs. Plenty of other fetch dogs—Chesapeake Bay, curly-coated, and flat-coated retrievers; and breeds such as Irish and American water spaniels and English springer spaniels and others, not to exclude mixed breed, unregistered dogs that also retrieve—grace the lives of countless people who seldom thumb through a dictionary.

This book, then, is a salute to retrievers and to the people who love them. So raise your cup and open these pages in toast to them all. And if you do so and notice a dog hair floating in your drink, you'll no doubt already have an inkling of what *Just Retrievers* will be about.

Len E. Lauber

P U P P Y   D A Y S

Puppy Days! Oh! puppy days!
Potlicker, rabbits and fun,
From dewey dawn to locust's song,
Nothing to do but run!

—Nash Buckingham, "My Dog Jim"

Where would you begin a book on retrievers, other than on the subject of puppies? It's a logical place to start, and let's face it: If you love retrievers of any age, you especially adore them as puppies. How can you not?

Just hold one. It's innocent, helpless, cuddly, and, oh! that warm, sweet smell of puppy fur. Gently press your nose into the pup's side. Inhale the intoxicating, doggy aroma; you know you're about to lose your heart again. Puppies know it too. It's part of the scam that they use to adopt us.

But let's get to mom and the rest of the litter. After all, we enter puppies' lives soon enough, and the first few weeks in any retriever's life must be devoted to family matters. Direct family, that is.

It starts with a chaotic transition from womb to whelping box. Put yourself in a puppy's place shortly before it enters the world: You're quite comfortable in otherwise confined quarters. The lights are out, so there's little trouble napping. You never feel hunger. You spend your days in dreamlike serenity. Suddenly, though, there's all this pushing and shoving–from brothers and sisters you know are close by but have never seen–and now you're lined up like paratroopers heading for an aircraft exit door. Wiggle. Strain. Geronimo!

Welcome to the outside world. For the first time, you feel cold, wet, and ravenous. No, there's no going back.

And there's an enormous tongue licking you!

9

A puppy's first days "on the outside," as chaotic as its birthday may have been, are anticlimactic. Suckle, sleep, snuggle with littermates. (Repeat as necessary to achieve desired results.)

Littermates. Bosom buddies, literally. At first they only know each other as fellow visitors at the milk bar who otherwise serve as handy pillows. Like piglets in a hay mow, they huddle together for warmth and security at nap time, which occurs a half dozen times between sunrise and dusk.

In about a week the little ones' eyes open, however, and behind each otherwise guileless, unfocused stare, you just know that trouble is brewing.

Puppies are seemingly helpless at this stage of life. Physically, that's true, but mentally they are planning a list of activities that their bodies can grow into. Their otherwise turtlelike movements will soon develop into tentative, wobbly steps. Coordinating and synchronizing four legs and feet isn't easy, though, and even a short stroll through the grass can wear a puppy out.

Self-expression gains new importance as the pups discover their vocal cords. Grunts, squeaks, wispy moans and sighs, laughable soprano barks, and comical growls work themselves into the pups' growing vocabularies. Competition rears its ugly head, too, and puppy toys are lusted over in a form of canine object envy.

Left: Jeff Drackers; center: William H. Mullins; right: Orion/International Stock

Left: Kent & Donna Dannen; right: Lee D. Salber; far right: Jeff Druckery

"Whoever said you can't buy happiness," Gene Hill once wrote, "forgot little puppies." Of course, when you lay down your money and bring the puppy home, the happiness is all yours, not the pup's. For the first time in its seven- to eight-week-old life, the puppy is away from mom and littermates. It finds itself in new surroundings, too, where everything and everyone smells different from the familiar and friendly environment in which it grew up. In his or her mind, it's just been kidnapped. As if weaning and the first trip to the vet weren't traumatic enough, adoption by a new human, from the pup's point of view, must be like being captured by aliens.

Like human infants, puppies need lots of affection. Like human infants, too, they need objects to see, smell, hold, and play with to help stimulate their mental development. Of course, this means a sufficient number of toys, ones the puppy can chew and carry around without hurting itself. How many toys are "sufficient"? Keep giving the puppy new ones until it lets you know it has enough. The puppy will eventually decide on a few favorite items, usually things that are yours.

Left: Gary Kramer; right: Sac Clay

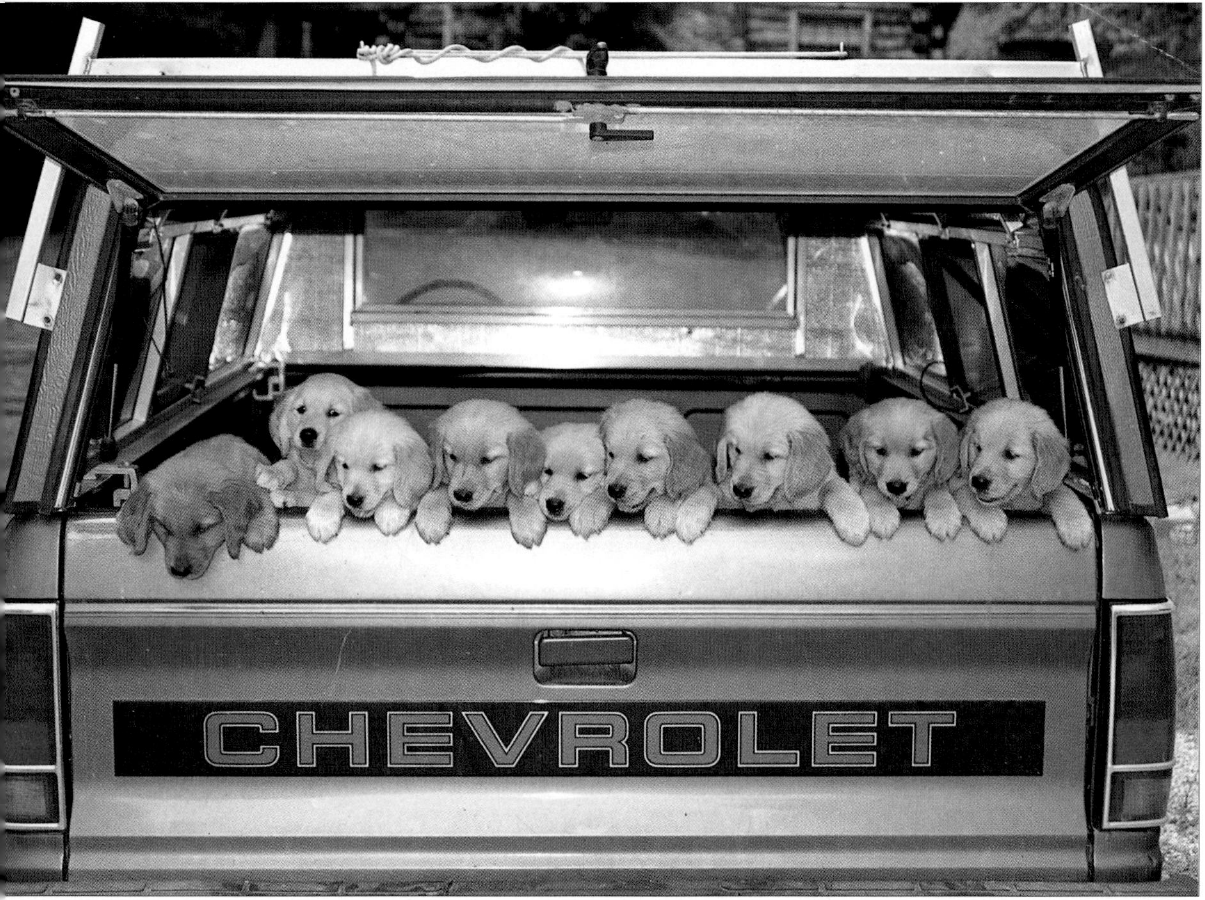
CHEVROLET

Minor spats, play, and mischief (described as family socialization by dog behaviorists) now become part of the daily ritual. This is how puppies learn that littermates are good for something other than comforters. The process also leads to new levels of doggy animation, especially roughhousing.

Far left: Henry H. Holdsworth/F-Stock; left: Heather R. Davidson; right: Close Encounters of the Furry Kind

Kids and puppies deserve each other. The late humorist Robert Benchley once said, "Every boy should have a dog. It teaches him to turn around three times before lying down." Best of all, having a puppy to play with nurtures a kid's compassion and his or her sense of responsibility for animals, something Nintendo games fail to convey.

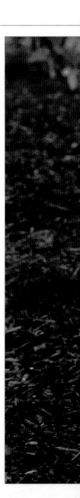

*T*he instinct triggers almost as soon as retriever puppies begin to walk. At first it's undirected activity—the puppy wanders about with something in its mouth—so perhaps, technically, it's not "retrieving." But then comes the day he chases that first tossed stick and brings it back to you, and you beam like a parent whose child has spoken its first intelligible word.

How long does a puppy remain a puppy? Some folks say nine months, others up to two years. But age is relative. Over the course of your dog's lifetime, as it ages from puppyhood to old age, you'll want to recall the days you nestled it in your arms like an infant. . . memories that will forever linger in your heart.

Far left: Close Encounters of the Furry Kind: left: Norma Behling; right: William H. Mullins

PEOPLE DOGS

*They'll stand between you and a stranger at the door, hackles raised,
rumbling a warning only a fool would ignore . . . two hours later, they'll be yapping at the
neighbor kids, trying to worm their way into a game of touch football.*

—Steve Smith, *Just Labs*

How many times have you heard it? Someone leans over to pet your dog and says, "I just love retrievers. They're such . . . people dogs." Most often, but not always, the ubiquitous compliment is directed toward a Lab. Since most retrievers of all types are genetically linked to the characteristically mellifluous Labrador, though, it's no wonder that retrievers in general share a tranquil, engaging temperament. They tolerate indignities foisted upon them by children. They endure taunts from the family cat (but not necessarily from the neighbor's cat). They love you unconditionally, crave your attention, sulk in your absence, and rejoice upon your return.

Yes, they do like people, with the possible exceptions of unfamiliar delivery men and suspicious visitors, who will be

duly warned exactly where a retriever's defense perimeter lies. The ferocious bark and defensive stance of a protective retriever present a formidable intruder alarm system. Only a fool might tempt fate by ignoring such a serious territorial warning, and if he does, he should be prepared to accept the consequences.

But the rumbling throat and raised hackles can instantly subside to an amicable *pet me, scratch me* solicitation once the retriever's owner introduces the dog to a heretofore unfamiliar house guest. Before long, the visitor may even be treated to some salubrious hand licking, a gesture of canine acceptance and goodwill. *Still,* the retriever will be thinking, staring softly into its new friend's eyes, *don't come around at night when the lights are out.*

27

I've always insisted that a retriever is not a pet; it's a companion, a pal. A canary is a pet. So is a hamster. Who ever heard of "people birds" or "people rodents"? Those critters don't go places with you, protect you, work for you or play with you. They sit in cages and generally don't give a damn about you, except at feeding time. A retriever, on the other hand, actually needs companionship, to be near its people. Gene Hill said it best: "We never really own a dog as much as he owns us."

28

Far left: Len E. Lauber; left: Chuck Pettie; right: Norvia Behling

Left: Norsia Behling; right: Chuck Perrie; far right: Dit Rutland

Around the house, a retriever will gladly engage in practices it wouldn't be caught dead doing in "dog circles." How would it look to other retrievers, for instance, to be straddled by kids like a hobby horse, to lounge in front of the fireplace with Elvis the cat or, worse, to frolic with Tabby in the backyard? Undignified. Fun, yes, but conspicuously undignified.

31

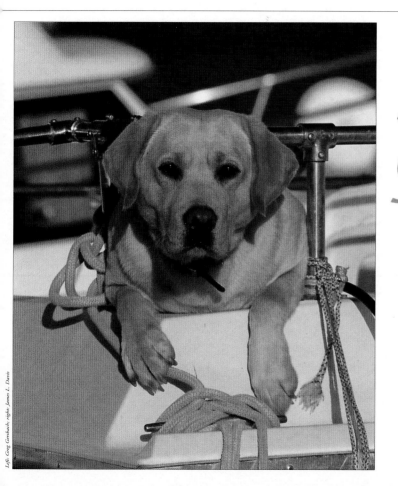

Left: Greg Gersbach; right: James L. Davis

You can make them sit, lie down, and stay. They'll do it if you say so, even if they prefer doing something else. It's not natural, after all, for a retriever to remain static, even temporarily, especially when there's so much important work to be done—stuff that has to be sniffed out, places that need exploring, boundaries that must be marked and picketed. There's just no end to a retriever's responsibilities, and how can they be accomplished if the dog is not on the move?

Every dog deserves a child. Left alone, both become easily bored, but put the two together and they'll readily entertain each other. This keeps the dog-child duo out of most types of mischief while providing each with healthy exercise. If you have a retriever but don't have a child for it to play with, have one, or at least borrow one. You owe it to your retriever.

Left: Lon E. Lauber; top right: Chuck Petrie; lower right: Norris Behling

35

Retrievers are doers. They're not content to sit at home alone. They need action and they want—often insist—you to take them along wherever it is you're going. To the grocery store. On a hike. To the shooting range. Roller blading. As long as they're with you, the place and activity don't really matter.

Far left: Kent & Donna Dannen; left: Kent & Donna Dannen; right: Becky Mills ; far right: Chris Dorsey

Look into the eyes of a retriever and you'll find a sentience unique among dogs. Maybe that's a statement only a retriever fan will embrace, but I firmly believe it. You'll learn to detect your dog's mood by its facial expressions, especially by searching its eyes. This familiarity is cultivated over time, and the dog will become better at it than you will. Have you ever glanced away from whatever absorbed your attention, glimpsed at ol' Sparky, and caught him staring at you? Were you feeling melancholy or downhearted? Did he stroll over to you and gingerly lay his head in your lap?

Far left: Dale C. Spartas/F-Stock; left: Len E. Lauber; right: Denver Bryan

Retrievers are like Boy Scouts: brave, loyal, dutiful, kind, and the other attributes scouts espouse but often grow out of later in life. Unfettered by human foibles, retrievers are free to remain true to their code of conduct. And their reverence, deserved or not, is reserved for the only gods they fathom. Us.

Left: Diane Jolie; right: Kent & Donna Dannen

F E T C H   I T !

He had as much fun in the water as any person I have known.
You didn't have to throw a stick in the water to get him to go in.
Of course, he would bring back a stick to you if you did throw one in.
He would even have brought back a piano if you had thrown one in.

— James Thurber, "The Thurber Carnival"

The big question is, Why do they do it? Sure, it's in their breeding, but that still doesn't explain why they enjoy doing it as much as they do. Throw the training dummy in the pond a dozen times and they'll swim after it a dozen times and get it for you. Throw a stick in the bushes and they'll plow through the shrubbery to find it. Throw the ball fifty times and they'll return it to you to throw a fifty-first time.

So why do they do it, and for whom are they retrieving these things: you or themselves?

The behavior of picking up objects—balls, sticks, game birds, Frisbees—and bringing them to their masters is a characteristic that makes retrievers distinct from other breeds and classes of

dogs. Not that other breeds don't retrieve: they do, but not with the finesse, heart, and aplomb exhibited by true retrievers. Retrievers are masters of the game, the fetch the essence of their existence. Retrievers commonly brave wave-swept estuaries and freezing marsh waters to retrieve fallen ducks; they'll leap from high embankments to retrieve a tossed stick; they'll challenge the most intimidating obstacle to retrieve the object of your desire. So, yes, it must be in the breeding . . . and in their hearts, and in the will, if not the need, to please us, first, and then themselves. But it still doesn't explain how they teach us to throw the ball fifty-one times.

43

Left: Lon E. Lauber; right: Diane Jolie; far right: Andy Anderson/F-Stock

*I*t doesn't really matter if it's a duck or pheasant, a stick or ball, a training dummy or an old shoe. They'll get it for you. If it lands in the water, all the better. This gives them a chance to get wet and maybe even a bit muddy— which they'll gladly share with you upon their return.

𝒥 To an anxious retriever, a water entry is analogous to what pilots describe as the safe landing of an aircraft— a controlled crash.

Left: David J. Sams/Texas Imprint; right: David J. Sams/Texas Imprint; far right: Chuck Perrie

Channeling natural ability into disciplined retrieving is rewarding but challenging. Most retrievers quickly learn to adapt to a training regimen and to comply with their master's commands. That is, if the trainer knows what he is doing and isn't confusing the dog or reprimanding it for mistakes made by himself, thus giving added meaning to the term "training dummy."

Another whack at Webster, who gives us this
definition: "Anthropomorphism: an interpretation of what
is not human or personal in terms of human or personal
characteristics, especially when incorrectly attributing
human values and senses to animals."

Give us a break, Noah, what you see here is *Enthusiasm*!

Far left: David J. Sams/Texas Imprint; left: David J. Sams/Texas Imprint; right: Marc Epstein; far right: Denver Bryan

*W*ith due regard to the many men who are talented retriever trainers, women are generally better at it. Why? Women are innately more patient, their voices more pleasant, their physical size and deportment less threatening. The teacher-pupil relationship is thus more conducive to learning. Looking back at my own grade school days, in fact, it was a woman who first motivated me to learn the alphabet . . . and to sit down on command.

Far left: William H. Mullins; left: William H. Mullins

Kent & Donna Dannen

Retrieving. It's cute. It's useful. The dogs love it, and so do we. Maybe, in its simplest context, it's a subliminal form of mutual gift giving. You toss the dog a gift, he gets it, and then he gives it back to you. You toss it again, he brings it back again. The gift that keeps on giving. Or you shoot a duck or pheasant or grouse for the dog. A gift from the sky! *How nice*, the dog thinks, *can I go get it?* "Sure," you say, and send him off. He comes back with it and, no longer knowing what to do with it, gives it to you, hoping all the while another feathered favor will fall from the heavens.

Sometimes, though, we're not involved in the equation, at least as the presenters of gifts. That is, the retriever will just go shopping for us. They're more than happy to do this. They'll bring us . . .

57

. . . things we want but haven't had time to get for ourselves

Left: Kent & Donna Dunston; right: Bill Kinney

. . . things we've forgotten

. . . things other hunters have gotten but weren't fast enough to get to themselves

Left: Michael A. Kelly; right: David J. Sams/Texas Imprint

. . . things nobody's gotten but were just floating in the lake

... things they think should interest us, and

. . . special things they're very proud of.

BRING ON
THE CLOWNS

*Every dog I've ever owned can easily be recalled to mind. Each
had a most distinct personality—a set of quirks, a philosophy, an
individual attitude toward life. Some were clowns . . .*

—Gene Hill, "The Cycle"

There's no reason to believe retrievers don't have a sense of humor. Anthropomorphic? Maybe, but anyone who thinks a dog can't share certain characteristics of humans is a poor observer of animal behavior, and especially retriever behavior. Besides, I thought we'd already settled the anthropomorphic thing. Sure, it's fair to say we sometimes see more humor in certain situations—like when we dress them up in funny hats and sunglasses—

than the retrievers do, but don't they have to have a sense of humor just to go along with our antics? (Or, maybe, they just think they look cool.)

Like some people, certain retrievers take life far too seriously, but others love to joke around, do goofy things, and even play pranks, on other dogs as well as people.

How about retrievers who like to take your things and hide them on you? Case in point: You're sitting on the living room floor, attaching new speakers to your stereo. You reach behind you for the screwdriver you set down a moment ago, and it's gone. You look over at Baxter, lying on his dog pillow ten feet away. "Hey, pal, what'd ya do with my screwdriver?"

The dog looks at you and cocks his head, his way of saying

What on earth are you talking about? He may even get up and help you search for the lost item, feigning interest but inwardly chuckling *Ha ha, no, that's not where it is* as you look behind the couch or under a chair. Then, as you lift up your buddy's floor pillow and the screwdriver comes into view, there's a sudden blur, a quick snatch, and the tool is gone again.

This disappearing-item game has happened to me more than once, and I've seen enough hats snatched off heads and little kids' pants wrestled down to their ankles by jovial retrievers and too many other pranks to believe that the dogs don't premeditate the whole thing.

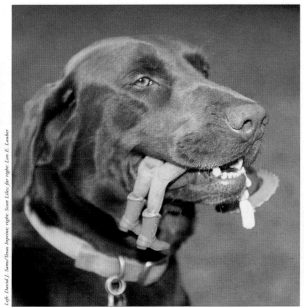

Back to Noah Webster for just a moment: "Clown: 1. a rude ill-bred person: BOOR 2: a fool, jester, or comedian in an entertainment (as in a play); specif: a grotesquely dressed comedy performer in a circus . . . ."

See what I mean? "Ill-bred"? "Boor"? Come on, Webster was a hopeless snob.

He probably owned a miniature poodle.

Left: Mark MacLeod; right: William H. Mullins; upper right: Dit Rutland

69

Comic retrievers display various levels of sophistication. This usually depends on the dog's preferred entertainment medium. Some extremely talented retrievers appear on TV and in movies and become so well known they have to disguise themselves in public places to avoid autograph seekers. Others, of lesser fame, may work as jesters with wandering minstrels. Most, God bless 'em, don't seek the limelight at all and are content to serve as humble country-style humorists.

Left: Photo Suntart/F-Stock; right: Chuck Petrie, far right: Larry Dahlemons

71

J"Jumping for joy" is a term that was probably coined by the owner of a happy retriever. There are times these canine comedians just can't contain themselves—they have to let it rip. Maybe, because they can't express themselves with laughter as we do, it's their way of cracking up at their own jokes.

Retrievers can entertain themselves (and us) at the drop of a hat—or the sweep of a snow shovel. Of course they know they can't really catch flying snow, but they'll keep trying to as long as you throw it. Anyway, if it's the only game at hand, you know they're going to clown around and play it.

All photos: Brent W. Phelps

GONE FISHIN'

*. . . when hauling fish from such a depth it is not unusual for
the fish to escape from the hook when at or near the surface of the water. A dog is kept on board for
retrieving the fish that break from the hook, and sometimes going underwater to do so.*

—Lord George Scott, from his personal letters

According to historical research into the origins of today's retrievers, their ancestors were working stiffs employed by fishermen in coastal Newfoundland as far back as the 1700s. The dogs were used to retrieve fish that slipped off of hooks or out of nets as they were hauled on board fishing dories. This function helped define form in the breeding of early retrievers, according to Richard Wolters. In his book *The Labrador Retriever*, Wolters explains: "Because the dog's job of retrieving fish and swimming lines had him in and out of the water, it follows that a . . . dog with an oily short coat (retaining less water) would serve best . . . So the early [fishing] crews needed a dog that was a strong swimmer, did not get coated

with ice, and could be handled in their dories to retrieve fish. A dog that could also find and retrieve the abundant waterfowl and upland game would be worth its weight in gold . . . "
Is it any wonder, then, that retrievers are still fishers today, two centuries later? Retrieving fish is as much in their breeding as is retrieving game. Both traits, it appears, were developed simultaneously. Evidently, the early retrievers led hard lives on Canada's maritime coast, and, hungry from hard labor and short rations, also fished alone (after work). The 1790s journals of English seaman Aaron Thomas contain this description: "They live chiefly on fish and many of these sturdy race fish for themselves. It is not a very uncommon thing to see

one of these dogs catch a fish . . . they go to the waterside and sit on a rock . . . the instant a fish appears they plunge into the water and seldom come up without their prey."

Unless you've taken a retriever fishing, you might suspect the accuracy of these historical accounts. But retrievers do retain a strong penchant for fishing, and they make great angling companions—they don't constantly offer advice on which is the correct bait to use, and when you describe to someone the dimensions of "the big one that got away," they'll never spill the beans on you.

Left: Denver Bryan; right: Denver Bryan

Unlike two centuries ago, when retrievers were required to fish for a living, they can now relax and assume a less assiduous role in the occupation. Still, while some retrievers today prefer the contemporary, contemplative approach to the endeavor, content to function as onlookers, others still feel a need to be . . .

. . . close to the action.

Far left: Mark Kayser; left: Denver Bryan; right: Bill Kinney

No, fishing is no longer a necessity for the modern retriever. The atavistic roots remain strong, however, and all retrievers retain an inherited sense of duty—to accompany their fisherman in his dory, to be at his side as he casts his net or hook upon the waters . . . and to still retrieve his fish if necessary.

M A R S H   &   F I E L D

At some point in the dim and distant past, man quit kidding himself
and concluded that, as predators go, he left a lot to be desired....
To his credit, though, he had brains enough to recruit the dog as his ally.
It was one of the shrewdest moves Homo sapiens *ever made.*

—Tom Davis, *Just Goldens*

Retrievers, as we know them today, would not exist were it not for the hunter. More than two centuries of selectively breeding these dogs for specialized hunting traits not only established the physical characteristics of contemporary retriever breeds, it also imbued them with the behavior patterns we find so engaging and useful.

History tells us that early retrievers, bred specifically for that purpose, worked the estates of aristocratic European landowner-hunters, as they still do today, solely as retrievers of hare and game birds driven before the gun by human beaters. The precursors of these dogs were propagated for their hunting and fish-retrieving abilities by the rugged settlers of the coast of Newfoundland, who relied heavily on game and fish for sustenance. Today in North America, unconfined by pressures of subsistence living and free to allow our hunting a broad array of expression unconfined by aristocratic tradition, we've fully developed the retriever's ability and natural desire to find and flush a variety of upland game birds as well as to retrieve waterfowl.

Nonetheless, not all retrievers attain the stature as hunters as do other individuals of their breed. To most hunters, that doesn't matter. A retriever to them is more a hunting partner than an extension of their shotgun, and each dog the hunter shares his life with leaves with him discrete memories of individual style, of grace—or lack thereof—and of

89

special character. Each dog, too, is remembered

singularly for the quality of its companionship.

And if the dog becomes an excellent hunter

too, all the better, for it is in the marsh and in

the field that retrievers make their own legends

. . . and become our heros.

Far left: Marc Epstein; center: Chuck Petrie; left: David J. Sams/Texas Imprint

Animal experts say dogs can't anticipate coming events. Those folks should spend a day in a duck marsh with an experienced retriever. The dog knows very well what's coming and where it's coming from, if not exactly when it will arrive. Experienced waterfowlers know they need not watch the sky for oncoming ducks—their retrievers' eyes and actions will tell them when it's time to get ready.

Among the hunting breeds, retrievers are renowned for their hardiness. Their insulative, water-resistant coats allow them to withstand harsh outdoor conditions. But there's more to it than that: They're also warmed by their desire to hunt and to accompany their masters afield, no matter the temperature, no matter icy, wind-driven waves, no matter rain, sleet, or snow. Like the postman, you know they'll be there.

Mike Barlow

When the shadows lengthen in a hunter's life, his thoughts should return to marsh and field and to the retrievers who loved and served him. It will lighten his heart to know those memorable friends await him now, as they did then, in unforgettable places where their spirits eternally dwell.